The Hidden Curriculum and Other Everyday Challenges for Elementary-Age Children With High-Functioning Autism

The Hidden Curriculum and Other Everyday Challenges for Elementary-Age Children With High-Functioning Autism

**Haley Morgan Myles and
Annellise Kolar**

PUBLISHING

P.O. Box 23173
Shawnee Mission, Kansas 66283-0173
www.aapcpublishing.net

PUBLISHING

©2013 AAPC Publishing
P.O. Box 23173
Shawnee Mission, Kansas 66283-0173
www.aapcpublishing.net

Publisher's Cataloging-in-Publication

Myles, Haley Morgan.

The hidden curriculum and other everyday challenges for elementary-age children with high-functioning autism / Haley Morgan Myles and Annellise Kolar. -- 2nd exp. ed. -- Shawnee Mission, Kan. : AAPC Publishing, c2013.

p. ; cm.

ISBN: 978-1-937473-10-5
LCCN: 2013933403
Previous ed. titled: Practical solutions to everyday challenges for children with Asperger syndrome. c2002.
Edition statement from cover.
Summary: Everyday tips for getting along at home, at school and in the community.
Audience: Children with autism spectrum disporders and their parents and teachers.

1. Children with autism spectrum disorders--Life skills guides--Juvenile literature.
2. Asperger's syndrome--Patients--Life skills guides--Juvenile literature. 3. Social skills in children--Study and teaching. 4. [Asperger's syndrome--Life skills guides. 5. Autism--Life skills guides. 6. Interpersonal relations.] I. Kolar, Annellise. II. Title.

RJ506.A9 M95 2013
618.92/858832--dc23   1303

NOTE:

The chart on page 41 is from *Successful Problem-Solving for High-Functioning Students With Autism Spectrum Disorders* by Kerry Mataya and Penney Owens, copyright 2013. Shawnee Mission, KS: AAPC Publishing. Used with permission.

The chart on page 42 is from *The Incredible 5-Point Scale – The Significantly Improved and Expanded Second Edition – Assisting Students in Understanding Social Interactions and Controlling Their Emotional Responses* by Kari Dunn Buron and Mitzi Curtis, copyright 2012. Shawnee Mission, KS: AAPC Publishing. Used with permission.

This book is designed in Helvetica Neue.

Printed in the United States of America.

Dedication

would like to dedicate this book to all the kids who can use a little extra help every day and can be anything they want to be. I would also like to thank my mom, my dad, my friend Annellise, Kirsten McBride, and Vivian Strand for their support in bringing about this second edition.

Introduction

Hi kids!

A lot of things have changed since I first wrote this book, which is why my friend Annellise and I decided to write some new helpful hints. We hope this book helps you with friends, school, and everyday activities. Remember that we learn something new every day, and we hope this book can help you do that.

Haley

Table of Contents

School-Related..1

1   Tests...1
2   Making Homework Easier and Fun 2
3   Asking Questions in Class...2
4   Redoing Work That You Got a Bad Grade On 3
5   Learning How to Do Something You Don't Enjoy 3
6   Remembering Things... 4
7   If You Forget Your School Lunch 5
8   Having Problems Doing Your Homework..................5
9   If You Need Help With Schoolwork When The Teacher
     Is Busy With Someone Else......................................5
10 Following Directions 6
11 Walking in Hallways at School.................................6
12 Recess 6
13 Fire Drills 7
14 Eating Lunch 7
15 Talking to Your Teacher...8
16 Working With Classmates..8
17 Cheating...9
18 If You Forget Your School Supplies.........................9
19 If You Forget to Turn in Your Homework 10
20 Show and Tell...10
21 Miscellaneous Classroom Rules 11

Getting Along 13

1   Listening...13
2   How to Dress for Special Occasions......................13
3   If You Break Something by Accident......................14
4   If Things Are Not Returned in Time 14
5   Keeping Promises.. 15
6   How to Handle Someone Who Brags and Shows Off............ 15
7   Forgiving a Friend 16

8   Proper Telephone Behavior 17
9   What to Do if You Are at a Party and Don't Know
     Anyone There..18
10 Being Respectful...18
11 How to Introduce Somebody 19
12 How to Make Your Friend Comfortable......................19
13 Following Rules... 19
14 Knowing What to Touch and Not Touch....................20
15 How to Start a Conversation 20
16 If You Receive a Gift You Don't Care For...................21
17 If You Receive Something as a Present That You
     Already Have.. 21
18 Spills..21
19 Going to a Wedding 22
20 Formal Parties..22
21 Birthday Parties 23
22 Building a Friendship 24
23 Telling Jokes..25
24 Eating Out 25
25 Manners While Eating 26
26 Favors 27
27 Having a Conversation 27
28 If Your Friend Seems Upset......................................27
29 Talking With Friends...28

Emotions and Concerns 29

1   Worrying About Things You Shouldn't Be Worrying About......29
2   Fears 29
3   Homesick 30
4   Feelings..30
5   Getting Upset...30
6   Afraid of Thunderstorms...31
7   Being Excited 31
8   If Someone Hurts Your Feelings 32
9   What to Do When You're Angry, Sad, or Your Feelings
     Have Been Hurt 32

10 Officer Dave's Safety Tips 33
    • Calling "911"...33
    • Smelling Smoke..33
    • Fire 33
    • Drugs...34
    • Car Safety 34
    • Leaks and Broken Water Pipes 34
    • Electrical Sparks 35
    • If the Lights Go Out 35
    • Dangerous Animal 35
    • Tornado 36
    • Hurricane 36
    • Broken Glass 36
    • Guns...37
    • Knives 37
    • If Someone Is in a Fight...37
    • Staying Away From Strangers...37
    • If Someone Knocks on the Door or Rings the Doorbell
       While You Are Home Alone..38
    • Bullies..38
    • If You Are Stuck in an Elevator 38
    • Internet Safety 39
    • Chatting Online..39
    • Putting Photos Online...39
    • Tattling vs. Being Responsible 39
11 Jealousy 40
12 Becoming Overwhelmed 40
13 Solving Problems...40
14 Getting a Handle on How You Are Feeling.....................41

First Aid...43
1 If You Get a Cut...43
2 Sick Pet...43
3 Splinter 44
4 Bites 44
5 Broken Bones 45

6   Choking 45

7   If You Lose a Tooth 45

8   Infection 46

9   Nose Bleed 46

10 If Your Feet Hurt 46

11 Injured Animal 47

12 Stings 47

13 What to Do if You Find Someone Who Is Hurt 47

Miscellaneous 49

1   Getting Lost in a Store 49

2   Sharing Things With Your Brother or Sister 50

3   Wanting to Stay up Late 50

4   If You Are Locked out of Your House 51

5   If You Can't Find Something You Are Looking For 51

6   If You Get Hungry 52

7   Home Alone 52

8   If You Are Lonesome 52

9   How to Keep Yourself Busy in a Car or on an Airplane 53

10 If Your Pet Gets Lost 53

11 Picking Up Your Toys 54

12 If You Find Something That Does Not Belong to You 54

13 Bedwetting 55

14 Trouble Finding Things or Being Organized 55

15 Something Bothers Your Senses 55

16 Someone Asks You to Do Something Mean or Bad 56

17 Bathroom Protocol 56

18 At the Doctor's Office 57

19 Waiting In Line 58

Your Own Ideas 59

School-Related

TESTS

Everyone takes tests. Sometimes you might worry when you have to take a test. Study, focus and, on the day of the test, eat a good breakfast. Scientists have discovered that students who eat a good breakfast do better in school. If you get nervous when the test is given to you, say to yourself, "I can do this!" Take a deep breath before you start. If you can't think of an answer to a problem, skip it and come back to it later.

If you have a hard time writing, ask the teacher if you can use a computer to type the answers or if you can tell the teacher the answers without having to write them down.

2 MAKING HOMEWORK EASIER AND FUN

To get some variety and maybe even learn better and faster, change the way you do homework sometimes. Do your homework using a gel pen instead of a pencil, or type your answers using a computer. You can also invent ways to make games out of learning! For example, instead of doing flashcards the old way, try to play "Go Fish" with a friend. You can play "Go Fish" to learn addition, subtraction, multiplication, or division. If you are learning to add, you can ask your partner for 3+2, and your partner will give you a card with the number 5 on it. You can check your answer with a calculator.

You can also take turns playing games and working; for example, you can work for 15 minutes and then play for about 10 minutes. It is best to do the work you don't want to do first instead of worrying about it. Just try to think about doing it in a different way. I love inventing new things. How about trying your ideas soon?

3 ASKING QUESTIONS IN CLASS

If you want to ask a question in class, raise your hand. If the teacher doesn't come to you after a bit, walk up to the teacher and say, "Excuse me, I have a question." If the teacher still doesn't answer, say it again louder. If you can't explain the question clearly, write it down on a sheet of paper and ask yourself if you understand the question yourself. If not, try writing the question again in different words. If rewriting the question isn't working, do something else for a couple of minutes to take your mind off it and try again.

4 REDOING WORK THAT YOU GOT A BAD GRADE ON

If you get an assignment back from your teacher with a bad grade on it and your teacher tells you to redo it, ask the teacher if there is an easier way for her to explain how to do the assignment, or ask her to show you again how to do the problem. The teacher will probably say yes. Learn how to do it, and BINGO you have it!

If you don't like to ask the teacher for help, think about what will happen. You will probably get a bad grade again because you still don't understand what to do. If you have a choice between discussing the problem with your teacher and getting a bad grade, what do you think you should do? Talk to the teacher! There you go!

5 LEARNING HOW TO DO SOMETHING YOU DON'T ENJOY

There are many things you can do for this problem. Try to make a game for each thing that you don't like to do. Here are two examples: If you don't like taking a bath, put a toy in the bathtub, like a rubber ducky. If you don't like to brush your teeth, try a new flavor of toothpaste or an electric toothbrush, etc., etc.

6 REMEMBERING THINGS

It is sometimes hard to remember things. Here are some ideas that might help you. Write the things you can't remember on a little card or a sticky note and put it in a place where you will see it each day. Pretty soon you will probably have memorized it.

If you cannot write, ask your parents to remind you what you are supposed to do at the proper time. For example, if you need to remember to wash your face before you go to bed, your parents can say, "Did you remember to wash your face?" just when you are about to go to bed.

You could also draw a picture to remind yourself. To remember to put lotion on your face before you go to bed, you could draw a figure of a soap man. His body would be a bar of soap and he would be holding a bottle of lotion. You could tape this to the mirror in the bathroom where you wash your face. If you can't remember to raise your hand in school, you can draw a little guy raising his hand or get a bendable figure who is raising her hand and leave it on your desk. If you get a bendable figure, it is probably not a good idea to mess with it while you are doing your work.

You can also do something fun to help you remember! Pretend that you can predict things! Every day, somebody who is forgetful comes in to see you. Tell the person the text on the card without read-ing it. If you are able to do it correctly, go on and try to remember another one!

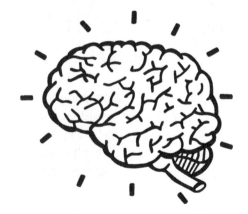

7 IF YOU FORGET YOUR SCHOOL LUNCH

If you are at school and forgot to pack your lunch, here are some solutions. Tell your teacher or the school secretary and ask them what to do. Usually, they will let you have a free lunch and you can pay them back the next day.

8 HAVING PROBLEMS DOING YOUR HOMEWORK

If you are doing your homework and can't figure out the answer to a problem, do something else for a couple of minutes. This will help you relax, and it sometimes helps you remember what you are supposed to do. If that still does not work, ask your parents or older brother or sister to help you.

9 IF YOU NEED HELP WITH SCHOOLWORK WHEN THE TEACHER IS BUSY WITH SOMEONE ELSE

If you need help and the teacher is with someone else, like another student or a teacher, skip the problem you are having difficulty with and go on to the next one. If it is okay with your teacher, ask your neighbor to help you. If you can't ask a neighbor, skip the problem and raise your hand to get help from the teacher. Don't get upset if you have to wait for a little while. If the teacher finishes with the other student or teacher and does not see that you have your hand raised, you can say, "Excuse me, can I have some help, please?"

10 FOLLOWING DIRECTIONS

If you don't understand the instructions somebody gives you for how to do something, ask the person to explain it an easier way. If it still doesn't help, ask him if he could write it down on a piece of paper. For example, if you don't understand directions at school, ask your teacher if she can explain it a different way, such as writing it down on the blackboard or showing you an example. If she is with someone else, don't forget to raise your hand to show that you need help. It is okay if you don't understand as long as you ask for help.

11 WALKING IN HALLWAYS AT SCHOOL

The hallways at school can be noisy and crowded. When walking to class, try to keep your hands down to your sides so that people can pass you more easily. If you are in a hurry and people are standing in front of you, it is never appropriate to push them aside. Simply say, "excuse me," and wait until they move out of the way so you can continue walking. If a friend meets up with you in the hallway and wants to talk, try to walk next to him if the hallway isn't very crowded. It usually isn't polite to walk in front of or behind another person if you are talking to him.

12 RECESS

Recess is a great time to play with your friends and classmates. Some common games are tag and hide-and-seek. When playing tag, it is important to touch the other person softly so you don't hurt her. During hide-and-seek, close your eyes and slowly count to 10 before you start looking for your classmates.

If you don't understand the rules of a game, ask your friends or your teacher to explain. A good thing about playing games with your friends is that it doesn't really matter who wins or who loses. Kids play games during recess to enjoy time with classmates, not to win. Whether or not you win, it is a good idea to say "good game" to friends at the end of recess. This means that you had fun and that it isn't important who wins or who loses. If there are swings or other playground equipment at your school, share with others so everyone can have fun.

Remember that although you can be loud during recess, it is important to be quiet when you return to class.

13 FIRE DRILLS

Schools usually have fire drills a few times a year to make sure students are prepared if a fire should ever happen. During a fire drill, a loud alarm will probably go off and your teacher will lead all the students out of the classroom to a safe place outside. If the alarm is too loud, you can cover your ears until you get outside. A fire drill is not a good time to talk to friends or ask your teacher questions. If you have to go to the bathroom, wait until the fire drill is over.

14 EATING LUNCH

The lunchroom at school can be a loud and busy place. When it is time for lunch, start to eat as soon as possible. After you get your food, sit next to your friends and

start eating so you don't waste time. Although other people may be talking loudly in the lunchroom, try to speak to your friends in an indoor voice. It is not polite to shout to kids across the room. Also, never throw food in the lunchroom, even if your friends are doing it.

15 TALKING TO YOUR TEACHER

It is very important to treat your teachers with respect. It is not okay to talk to teachers the same way you talk to your friends. Try to use a pleasant voice when talking to your teachers and avoid making rude comments about them, even if you disagree with them at times. If you disagree with your teacher, it is okay to nicely say what you think or, better yet, wait to talk to your teacher after class.

Sometimes teachers send you messages without actually talking. For example, if your teacher clears her throat and crosses her arms, it is usually a sign that she wants you to pay attention to her. Maybe she will give you directions or wants you to be quiet. If you don't understand what your teacher is trying to communicate using this kind of body language (clearing throat, crossing arms), politely ask her to explain it to you.

16 WORKING WITH CLASSMATES

When you are working in a group, you are supposed to share the work. Don't do all the work, even if the other kids aren't doing it the same way you would and you don't think they are doing as good a job as you. Remember, everyone is supposed to learn from group projects so everybody has to do their share.

Sometimes the teacher may say it's okay for you to help other students if you understand a problem or assignment. When you are helping someone, be nice, and don't say mean things about their work. Also, don't take their paper and write in the answer. Kids will think you are rude and cheating.

17 CHEATING

Cheating is bad. Never copy a classmate's work during a test, even if you don't know the answer. Sometimes you are helping someone cheat without even knowing it. If you let someone look at your paper and copy the answer, you are letting them cheat. If your teacher finds out, you might get a bad grade. If you notice anyone cheating, tell your teacher quietly after class. Otherwise, you will likely be called a tattle-tale.

18 IF YOU FORGET YOUR SCHOOL SUPPLIES

If you forget your supplies at home, such as a pen or a notebook, it is not okay to just sit and do nothing. Ask the teacher if he has an extra pen or paper you may borrow for class. Calmly explain that you forgot yours at home and will return the teacher's pen or paper later.

If the teacher does not have any, ask a friend in your class. Be extra careful with other people's things. They won't let you borrow their things again if you ruin them.

19 IF YOU FORGET TO TURN IN YOUR HOMEWORK

If you forget to turn in your homework when you are supposed to, make sure that you give it to the teacher as soon as you remember. If you tend to forget turning in your homework, you might want to have your teacher or parent help you create a folder just for homework. You can label the left side of the folder as "Homework To Do" and the right side with "Homework To Turn In." That way, all of your homework will be in one spot, and it will be easier to remember to turn it in (hopefully, it will also help you to remember to do it).

20 SHOW AND TELL

Sometimes your teacher might ask you to bring something to class to share – to show and talk about – with your classmates. It may be a toy, a photo, or a story about something you saw or did. When your classmates are talking about their item, don't ask them questions. Wait until the teacher tells you it is time to ask questions and remember to raise your hand. Otherwise, you might miss something important that your classmate is trying to say.

21 MISCELLANEOUS CLASSROOM RULES

Here are a few helpful classroom rules:
- Don't be late to class.
- If you want to use someone else's supplies, ask them first.
- If your teacher asks another student to be quiet, you can assume that you should be quiet, too.
- If your teacher says you should stop doing a certain activity, it does not necessarily mean you are in trouble. The teacher is just giving you a warning. However, if you continue doing the same activity, you can get in trouble.
- Most schools don't allow you to chew gum in school or pass notes. If you do these things, you can get in trouble.
- If a teacher is talking, listen to her and try to look at her face. This shows the teacher that you respect her.
- When saying the Pledge of Allegiance, try to keep still and look at the flag.

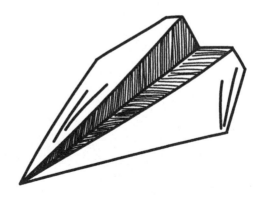

Getting Along

1 LISTENING

If someone is talking, it is polite to listen. If you look at the person who is talking, he or she will know that you are listening. If someone talks for a long time about a subject that you are tired of, or not interested in, you can say, "Excuse me, can I talk now, please?" or "Can we talk about something else?"

2 HOW TO DRESS FOR SPECIAL OCCASIONS

If you are going to a party or some other special occasion and don't know what to wear, ask your parents or a friend who will be there too what she/he is wearing. It is important to be clean and to try to look your best.

3 IF YOU BREAK SOMETHING BY ACCIDENT

If you break something, some parents want you to tell them right away. Other parents may want you to clean up the mess before you tell them. You know best what the rule is in your family. Always apologize for breaking the item.

If you break something at someone else's house, tell the person, say you are sorry, and offer to help clean up the mess. To show how sorry you are, you might offer to replace the item you broke.

4 IF THINGS ARE NOT RETURNED IN TIME

If you let somebody borrow something and they don't return it, ask if you can get your object back. If the person thinks that he had it only for a little while, think about it. Maybe he had the item only for three days or so. If that is not the case, tell your mom and dad about it. They can probably help.

If you get an object returned, such as a stuffed animal or a favorite sweatshirt, and it is dirty, tell the person who borrowed it in a polite way to clean it. If they still return it dirty, don't let them borrow your stuff again. If someone borrows something such as a baseball card or an American Girl card and ruins it, don't loan them anything again until they replace or pay for the damaged item.

5 KEEPING PROMISES

Sometimes, it is hard to keep promises. Here are some tips on keeping promises. (1) Don't make promises quickly. (2) Before you make a promise, think about it. Will it be hard to keep? Can you do it? (3) If someone else makes a promise and breaks it for a special reason, forgive them. For example, if your dad promises to take you camping and on the day of the camping trip he breaks his arm and can't take you, that is not really breaking a promise. Your dad cannot help it.

6 HOW TO HANDLE SOMEONE WHO BRAGS AND SHOWS OFF

If someone shows off, ignore it. For example, if your friend says, "Look at how many trophies I have. I have more than anyone," say, "That's nice" and try to talk about something else.

Some people like to talk about them-selves all the time like, "I won last year's race. I won this year's race. I have millions of trophies and I just won a race now." If the bragging gets worse, talk to your parents or your teacher. They usually have good advice. If they don't have any helpful suggestions, try to ignore the irritating behavior or stay away from the per-son, if possible. If you like the person and would like to stay friends, you might just need to tell him that he is talking about himself too much and that bragging is not nice. Tell him that there are other things to talk about and give him a few examples.

7 FORGIVING A FRIEND

If your friend is angry with you and you don't know what you did or said wrong, think about it. Pretend that you are your friend, and think about what you said. Would you be happy if someone said that to you? Do you now feel sorry? If not, here is another idea. You can write a note to your friend explaining what happened and maybe say you are sorry.

If you are angry with a friend because of something she did, tell her how you feel. If you cannot do that, try to write about something you like. That should keep your mind off her. If that does not work and you are still angry, it is time to ask your parents for advice.

Here is an example of what happened to me once. I told my friend Abby that I didn't like the way Lily always bragged about herself. Abby told Lily, and I felt bad because (1) I was telling Abby a secret and she didn't keep the secret and (2) I didn't want to hurt Lily's feelings even though I didn't like her bragging. I was angry with Abby for a little bit, but then I forgave her. I also thought that I probably should not be saying something about Lily that might be a little mean.

8 PROPER TELEPHONE BEHAVIOR

- **HOW TO START A PHONE CONVERSATION**
  If you are talking to a person you know, start out by saying, "Hi, this is (your name)." Then you can ask, "How are you doing?" or "What is going on?" If the person on the other end can't think of anything to say, it is your turn to talk! Talk about something that is going on at your house or maybe about a TV show you have seen, a new toy, etc., etc.

- **HOME ALONE**
  If the phone rings when you are home alone and you and your parents have decided that it is okay for you to answer it, ask who is calling and tell them that your mom or dad is not available to come to the phone right now. Do not say that your mom or dad is not home. Don't forget to get the person's telephone number and take a message. It is best if you repeat back the name, phone number, and what the person wanted before you hang up.

  If your family has an answering machine, sometimes it is a good idea just to let incoming calls go to the answering machine when you are home alone.

- **OBSCENE PHONE CALLS**
  If you ever receive an obscene phone call, hang up immediately. Write what time the person called and what he or she said. If there's more than one call, do this every single time. Tell your parents or another adult immediately.

- **ANSWERING MACHINE**
  If you call somebody and get an answering machine, be sure to speak especially clearly and slowly. Leave your first and last name, the name of the person you want to reach, and your telephone number.

9 WHAT TO DO IF YOU ARE AT A PARTY AND DON'T KNOW ANYONE THERE

If you are at a party, Scouts or anywhere else and don't know anyone, look for someone who you think it would be nice and interesting to meet, or look for somebody who also seems to be alone. Walk up to that person and say "Hi!"

If the person seems to ignore you, say "Hi!" again, but louder. If the person still does not answer, try to find someone else to talk to. Say, "Hi!" and tell the person your name. Ask them questions about their interests, pets, etc. Tell jokes, talk about the latest musical group, etc., etc.

10 BEING RESPECTFUL

Be respectful because it makes other people feel good. It also might make you feel good. Here are some ways that I have learned to be respectful: (1) look at people directly when you are listening to them and try not to interrupt; (2) say "please" and "thank you"; (3) treat other people's things as special as you would treat your own things; (4) don't brag or show off; and (5) say nice things. If you have guests over, being respectful means that you ask them what they would like to do first. Then you can do what you want second.

11 HOW TO INTRODUCE SOMEBODY

When you need to introduce someone to a friend or relative, introduce the oldest person first. For example, if John is your uncle and Mary is your friend, say, "Uncle John, this is my friend Mary. Mary, this is my Uncle John."

12 HOW TO MAKE YOUR FRIEND COMFORTABLE

If your friend is new to your house, show him around. If your friend is staying for a while, ask if he wants a drink or a snack if you know that's okay with your parents. Take turns playing games with each other. Have fun!

13 FOLLOWING RULES

Follow the rules so you don't get into trouble. Sometimes you may not like a rule that your teacher or parents set. If you don't like the rule, ask them if you can compromise. If it is impossible to compromise, try to follow the rule even if it is hard. You usually get used to following the rule eventually.

Most parents make rules to keep you safe. Sometimes it is hard for kids to understand that. When you get to be a parent, you will probably have the same type of rules for your kids and your kids will probably not like the rules either.

14 KNOWING WHAT TO TOUCH AND NOT TOUCH

Sometimes it is hard to know what to touch or not to touch when you see something interesting in a shop, in somebody's house, etc.

Here are a couple of solutions. Pretend that you own the thing that you want to touch so badly. Would you let someone touch it? If you think so, you can probably touch it. If not, don't touch it. If you are still not sure, here are a couple of other ideas. If there is glass covering the item, don't touch it! If there is a rope in front of it, as there sometimes is in museums and stores, don't touch it! If you are still in doubt, ask someone you trust.

15 HOW TO START A CONVERSATION

If it is a person you don't know, start out by saying, "Hi, my name is (add your name)." Talk about a popular band, the weather, jokes, etc. If you know the person, say, "Hey, (add the other person's name)" and talk about things that you both enjoy and already know about each other.

16 IF YOU RECEIVE A GIFT YOU DON'T CARE FOR

Thank the person who gave it to you, even if you don't care for the gift. You can always exchange it, or never use or wear it. Say, "Thank you very much for the (name of the gift)" and add something nice about the gift, such as, "Pink is one of my favorite colors." Never tell the person that you don't like the gift. It would hurt their feelings. If it's an item of clothing, wear it when you invite the person over who gave you the gift.

17 IF YOU RECEIVE SOMETHING AS A PRESENT THAT YOU ALREADY HAVE

If you get a gift of something you already have, you can exchange it for something else. Thank the person for the gift. Don't make any bad faces or say anything impolite. If you think about it, the gift was the perfect gift. The person thought you would like it — and you do. You just already have it. You can say, "Thank you very much for (name of gift)" or "I really like the (name of gift)."

18 SPILLS

If you spill something, tell an adult that you are sorry and try to clean it up. Don't get upset. It is okay if you spill a little. Everyone spills something once in a while.

19 GOING TO A WEDDING

If you are invited to a wedding, talk to your parents about what to wear – something that is comfortable, but fancy is best. Be quiet during the ceremony. When the bride throws the bouquet of flowers, if you are a girl, you may want to jump, but don't wrestle with others to get it. If the guests dance after the wedding, you can dance, too! Have fun! Sometimes there is  a place at the party where kids can hang out with toys, electronics, and more. If you get bored and you don't have anything to do, be patient and remind yourself that the wedding will soon be over.

20 FORMAL PARTIES

If you are going to a formal party, talk to your parents about what to wear – something that is comfortable but fancy usually works best. Be very polite (see BEING RESPECTFUL, page 18). Bring a book or a small toy along in case you get bored.

21 | BIRTHDAY PARTIES

If a friend of yours is celebrating a birthday and he hasn't asked you to come to the party, don't invite yourself. If he doesn't invite you, it doesn't necessarily mean he doesn't want to be your friend. Try not to take it personally.

If you are invited to a birthday party there are some rules you will want to follow.

- After being invited to a party, try not to talk about the party around people who weren't invited. It is rude, and you don't want to make other people feel left out.

- It is a good idea to bring a gift for your friend. Try to find a gift that you are sure your friend will like. Remember, you and your friend may have different tastes in gifts. Even if you think a present is great, your friend might not agree with you.

- Normally, a birthday cake is served with candles on top. Let the birthday boy or girl blow out the candles and don't start eating cake until others have started.

- If you don't like the food or cake that is being served, don't hurt the host's feelings by saying you don't like it. A more appropriate response would be "No, thank you" or "I'm not very hungry right now." Remember, you can get food that you like after the party.

- After eating cake, the birthday boy or girl normally starts opening presents. Don't tell how much money you spent on a gift. Also, don't make rude comments about gifts that others brought, even if you think that they aren't good gifts.

- You might not like everything about the birthday party. Maybe you won't like the party decorations or the flavor of the cake. Maybe you will think your own birthday party was better. Don't say these things to your host. He or she probably chose the cake and decorations and is really happy with the party.

Overall, a birthday party is a chance to meet new people, celebrate your friend, and maybe eat some good food, too. Have fun!

22 BUILDING A FRIENDSHIP

Building a friendship can take time. A good way to start a new friendship is to introduce yourself or start a conversation with a classmate (see page 20 – How to Start a Conversation). You can talk about things that you enjoy doing, and if the conversation goes well, a friendship may develop. The next step in developing a friendship could be to invite each other to play. With your parents' permission, you can invite a classmate over to your house. Another option is to go to the movies or to go bowling together. The good thing about these kinds of activities, especially at the beginning of a new friendship, is that they have a specific starting and ending point. Besides, if thinking of something to talk about is difficult for you, that issue is partly solved also.

A friendship means that both you and your friend do nice things for each other. That is, both of you take time to talk and play together. If you are nice to a classmate but she is mean to you, she is not your friend.

23 TELLING JOKES

It is not okay to say the same joke to the same person(s) over and over. A joke is usually only funny the first time. If you overhear your classmate telling a joke and you use the same joke he does, people will not think you are very funny because they have already heard the joke. There is a difference between laughing at a joke and laughing at someone. If someone is teasing another person and trying to hurt them, it is not okay to laugh.

24 EATING OUT

When eating out with your family or with a friend, certain "rules" and traditions apply. To make sure everybody has a good time, please keep the following in mind.

- Before leaving to go out to a restaurant, be sure to ask your parents about the dress code. If you are going to a formal restaurant, you may have to change your outfit.

- At most non-fast-food restaurants, you have to wait to be seated. After you arrive at your table, the waiter usually gives you a menu from which you order what you would like to eat. If you need

help understanding the menu, ask one of your parents or others at your table to explain the menu to you.

- Sometimes people order appetizers or "family-style" meals. This means that the food comes to your table on a large plate. When eating this kind of meal, don't eat directly off of the large plate. Place some of the food on your own plate before beginning to eat. Make sure everyone has had a helping before you have seconds.

- When several people order different things, everybody's food does not always come at the same time. Even if your food is served, try not to eat until everybody at the table has food in front of them.

25 MANNERS WHILE EATING

- It is not polite to start eating before everyone is sitting down and has their food. Some families like to say grace before the meal. While someone is saying grace, try to be quiet and still and don't begin eating until grace is over.

- While eating, remember to keep your mouth closed and try to talk only when you have no food in your mouth. If someone asks you a question when you are still chewing, you can hold up your pointer finger. This shows that you need a few moments to finish eating before you can talk.

26 FAVORS

If you do a favor for someone, they might not return the favor to you right away. Don't keep a tally of what favors you have done for people. Sometimes you just do a favor for someone because they are your friend, even if you don't get anything in return. Also, be sure to be understanding and reasonable when you ask someone for a favor, and thank people that help you.

27 HAVING A CONVERSATION

When you are having a conversation with someone, they will be upset if you interrupt them, even if you don't mean to. Sometimes, people pause while they are talking to take a breath or to think for a moment. If someone pauses, wait a few seconds before you start talking to make sure they are finished.

28 IF YOUR FRIEND SEEMS UPSET

If you notice that your friend is feeling bad, don't make fun of him or tell the whole class. That will make him feel worse. If you want to help, ask the person privately if there is anything you can do. He may ask you to simply listen while he explains what is bothering him. If he says there is nothing you can do, accept that answer and don't ask again as that could upset him further.

29 TALKING WITH FRIENDS

If you are with a group and are not adding to the conversation, others may think that you are not interested and may ignore you. If you don't know what to say, ask yourself, "What would the other kids like to talk about?" and talk about that. Or you can ask them a question like, "Have you seen any good movies lately?" or "What's your favorite video game?"

Emotions and Concerns

1 WORRYING ABOUT THINGS YOU SHOULDN'T BE WORRYING ABOUT

There are a lot of things that you should not worry about because they might not happen: (1) tornadoes, (2) hurricanes, (3) fire, (4) getting a bad grade on a test, (5) getting a disease, (6) not being first in line, or (7) spilling your milk during lunch. Try to think about happy things, not sad things. Instead of worrying about not being first in line to go to lunch, think of the good things that you will eat at lunch. Instead of worrying about getting a bad grade on a test, think about how proud you are of yourself that you will do your best.

2 FEARS

Everyone is afraid of something: the dark, missing the bus, make-believe creatures, etc. Ask your mom and dad what they were scared of when they were your age. Ask how they conquered their fears. It could help you.

3 HOMESICK

If you are at a friend's house and miss your parents, tell your friend's parents that you want to go home. Then call your parents and ask them to come and pick you up. Sometimes when you feel homesick, just talking to your parents will make you feel better, so you may not want to leave. Either way, it's okay.

4 FEELINGS

Share your feelings, but not too much or too little. For example, it is okay to say, "I'm really upset because (say what you are upset about)" so that people will know how you feel. It is probably not okay to repeat that three or four times in a row or have a tantrum. If you don't share your feelings, you may feel as if you have a hole in your stomach, and that hurts a lot. On the other hand, if you share your feelings too much, it may bore others. It is important to share your feelings with your family.

5 GETTING UPSET

If you feel like you are going to scream or yell, go to your room and punch your pillow, listen to music, draw, or do something else to calm down. If you get upset at school and feel like you are going to yell, tell your teacher that you would like to leave the classroom to calm down. Maybe you can go to the bathroom or take a short walk.

6 AFRAID OF THUNDERSTORMS

Don't be afraid of thunderstorms. If you like music, pretend that the rain is a drum, that the wind is a broken flute, etc. If you like sports, pretend a ball is hitting a bat when you hear thunder. If you like mechanics, pretend that the sounds you are hearing come from an old, noisy factory. Soon it will be fun listening to thunderstorms.

7 BEING EXCITED

If you are so excited about something special that is about to happen that you can't think of anything else, here are a couple of solutions to help take it off your mind: (1) Try to keep your mind off of it by staying busy and doing something you like. (2) Set a timer or alarm that will go off when the special event is going to happen. That way, you don't have to think about it in the meantime. (3) Ask your parents to let you know when the exciting thing is close to happening so that you can do something else that is fun while you are waiting. (4) Write in your diary about it. Sometimes writing in a diary can help you understand how you feel and make you calm or feel better and (5) Ask your parents for other ideas.

8 IF SOMEONE HURTS YOUR FEELINGS

If someone hurts your feelings, it is probably just an accident. But if it happens several times, tell your teacher or your parents and ask them what to do. If your parents' advice does not help, try to stay away from the person who is hurtful. Sometimes kids say things to hurt others' feelings because they don't feel good about themselves. It is hard to remember that when someone is calling you a name or teasing, so the safest thing is to stay away.

9 WHAT TO DO WHEN YOU'RE ANGRY, SAD, OR YOUR FEELINGS HAVE BEEN HURT

If you are angry or sad about something, talk with your mom or dad about it because they can usually help. If you are angry, it is usually not appropriate to scream, yell, or hit. Try to relax, think about something else, go to your room and punch your pillow, or do something else that can make you feel better. You usually will need to talk it over with the person who made you angry or sad, but make sure that you know what you want to say first. Don't say anything to hurt the other person's feelings; that won't help. You can practice what to say with your parents first.

10 OFFICER DAVE'S SAFETY TIPS

Not everybody is as lucky as I am to have an uncle who is a police officer. In this part I would like to share some of his advice for staying safe in many different kinds of emergencies or difficult situations.

- **CALLING "911"**

  Call "911" if there is an emergency. After you dial "911" and someone answers, say your first and last name, where you live, or where the emergency happened, your phone number, and what is wrong. Speak slowly and clearly so the operator can understand and take the necessary action to send help.

- **SMELLING SMOKE**

  If you ever smell smoke or dangerous fumes, tell everyone in the house. You need to have an escape plan to get out of the house. If your family does not already have a plan, suggest that you sit down and develop one. You might also want to get a carbon monoxide detector that will help detect dangerous fumes. See also FIRE

- **FIRE**

  If you smell smoke or there's a fire in your house, it is important that you and your family get out as soon as possible. If you are in your bedroom with the door closed, don't open it. Put the back of your hand on the door knob. If it is hot, do not open the door. Go to another door or go to the nearest window to get out

safely. When you open the window, don't jump if there is nothing soft to land on. If there is a tree nearby, climb down it as quickly as possible. If you are on the second floor and there is an elevator, don't go on the elevator. Go down the stairs. If you cannot do any of these things, yell and scream for help out of the window. If the door knob is cold, open the door and crawl to the nearest exit (door or window).

Get out as fast as you can. Don't go back in the house to get anything. Nothing is as important as your life. You can always get another book or toy later on if your things are damaged or lost in a fire. Make sure your fire alarm is working. It is good to check it every week. My uncle says, "Tuesday is test day." Change the battery every year on a day that you can remember, like your birthday or January 1.

- **DRUGS**
  If you find something that looks like drugs, pills, a syringe, etc., immediately tell your teacher, parent, or an adult you trust. Do not pick up, eat, or touch anything. If someone offers you drugs, say "No!" immediately, run away from the person, and tell what happened to an adult you trust.

- **CAR SAFETY**
  Make sure you always wear your seatbelt in the car. That way, if you are in an accident, you are less likely to get hurt. If you are under the age of twelve years old, always ride in the back seat because the air bags in the front could hurt you badly if you are in an accident. Always lock the doors.

- **LEAKS AND BROKEN WATER PIPES**
  If you notice water leaking from a pipe or faucet in your house, tell your mom or dad immediately because they may need to call a plumber, or

try to fix it themselves. If you don't like the sound of a faucet drip-ping, put a small towel or washcloth in the sink so you can't hear the sound, but make sure the water can still drain out so it won't overflow.

- **ELECTRICAL SPARKS**
  If you notice a spark from an electrical outlet or appliance, turn the appliance off. Don't unplug it. Tell an adult immediately. If a fire begins, see FIRE above for what to do.

- **IF THE LIGHTS GO OUT**
  If the power goes out in part of the house, your family may have too many electrical appliances plugged in at the same time, such as the toaster, microwave, TV, computer, air conditioner, etc. Don't tug on any cords because you might hurt yourself. If they haven't already noticed, tell your parents or another adult that the lights are out. They may have to put in a new fuse or reset the fuse box. If your whole neighborhood does not have electricity, it is probably a power outage, and the power company will have to fix it. If you are without power for a long period of time, you may have to stay with friends or relatives or in a hotel. I always keep a flashlight in my nightstand and we also have one in the kitchen.

- **DANGEROUS ANIMAL**
  Some animals that don't look dangerous may actually be dangerous. For example, a snake might look harmless but it could bite you. A mouse is small, but it might carry diseases. Don't touch the animal or go near it.
  Tell an adult you trust about it instead and ask for help. A good rule is not to touch an animal that is not yours unless you have permission by the owner. Don't touch wild animals unless they are in a petting zoo.

- **TORNADO**

  If a tornado hits your area, it is recommended that you get food and water and go to low ground, like a basement. If you don't have a basement, go to a bathroom in your house or a place that has no windows. Getting under a table is also a safe thing to do. Put cushions on you to protect yourself from falling glass or anything else that might cause damage to your body. If you are in a car and a tornado is coming, get out of the car with the adult and go to a deep ditch and lie down flat. Stay as close to the ground as possible. It is not safe to go in a car if you hear that a tornado is coming.

- **HURRICANE**

  If a hurricane hits, don't panic. Your family probably has a safety plan; if not, you may suggest that they develop one for the future. It is recommended that you get food, water and a raincoat. Go to high ground. You can also go to a hurricane shelter if there is one near you.

- **BROKEN GLASS**

  If you ever see broken glass, don't walk in it or touch it. If you break something and there is glass all over the floor, tell your parents or another adult. Be very careful when cleaning up, as tiny pieces of glass can be hard to see but can cut you badly. Sometimes your parents might not want you to clean up the pieces because they think you might get hurt. If that is the rule in your house, wait for your parents to clean up the broken glass and stay away from the area in the meantime.

- **GUNS**
  If you ever see a gun, don't mess with it! If someone is playing with it, tell the person to stop and immediately leave the area. If they ask why, say, "It is a weapon and can kill people." If they still don't stop, tell an adult you trust about it. Even if they do stop, you still need to tell an adult you trust!

- **KNIVES**
  If you ever see a person playing with a knife, tell them not to do it. If they ask why, tell them that knives are sharp. If they do not stop, leave the area and talk to an adult you trust. Never play with knives, and be careful using them. If you are cooking and need to use a knife, be very careful and make sure you know how to use it. If you are a beginner, it is best to start with a safety knife that can cut food, but not people. My mom bought me a safety knife so I could learn to cut and cook. Be safe!

- **IF SOMEONE IS IN A FIGHT**
  If kids are fighting with each other, tell them to stop. You probably don't want to jump in the middle of the fight because you might get hurt. Get help from an adult immediately. If you hear someone saying that they are going to be fighting later on, tell an adult. Ask the adult not to tell the kids that you said anything, because you don't want to get the reputation of being a tattle-tale.

- **STAYING AWAY FROM STRANGERS**
  If you are ever approached by a stranger in the street who wants you to go with him or her or wants you to help find a puppy in a store or any place else, don't respond but start running in the opposite direction. If there's somebody else nearby, go up to them

and ask for help or call out. Tell your parents or another adult about the stranger and ask for advice. You can always ask a police officer for help.

- **IF SOMEONE KNOCKS ON THE DOOR OR RINGS THE DOORBELL WHILE YOU ARE HOME ALONE**
  You and your parents probably have a rule about opening the door, especially when you are at home alone. If it is okay to open the door for certain people, it is a good idea to have a list of their names. If someone knocks on the door and you are the only one home, DO NOT open the door if the person's name is not on the list, even if you know the person. Look through the peephole. If you know who it is, write the person's name on a piece of paper so you can remember who came to the door and tell your parents later on.

- **BULLIES**
  Get away from anybody who is teasing or bullying you or your friends. If it is at school, tell your teacher or playground supervisor. If it happens after school, go in the opposite direction and be sure to tell your mom or dad exactly what happened when you get home. You can also ask a police officer about safety tips for dealing with bullies. If bullies want money, candy, or anything else, don't give it to them. If you do, they will probably pick on you again.

- **IF YOU ARE STUCK IN AN ELEVATOR**
  If you get stuck in an elevator, don't panic. There is usually an emergency phone or a red button to push in the elevator. Lift the phone and call, or push the red button. If there is neither of these, yell out loud. People will hear you.

- **INTERNET SAFETY**

  When you are online, it is not okay to tell people information about yourself or your family. Sometimes, people on the Internet lie to get personal information and use it to hurt you. Ask your parents what is okay to tell people online and what is not. If you are not sure if something is safe, don't say or write it.

- **CHATTING ONLINE**

  If you are on a website that allows you to comment on things or "chat" with other people, be very careful that nothing you say will hurt others. Something may seem funny to you, but other people reading it may think that it is mean. Since people in these kinds of online situations can't hear your voice, it is easy to misinterpret your meaning. Remember: It is a lot harder to apologize to someone you've made feel bad than it is to think about it before you say it. So think ahead.

- **PUTTING PHOTOS ONLINE**

  Sometimes, you may want to put pictures of you and your friends on the Internet to share with others. Remember that once you put the photos on the Internet, you might not have total control of who can see them. Don't share pictures that might make someone else feel bad or that you wouldn't want someone to see.

- **TATTLING VS. BEING RESPONSIBLE**

  There is a difference between tattling and being responsible. Sometimes, the things people say and do hurt others or get others in trouble. When people are saying or doing these kinds of things, it is important to tell an adult. You are not being a tattle tale; you are helping keep everyone safe.

11 Jealousy

Sometimes when a friend gets something you want, it is easy to be jealous. But instead of being upset, think about how happy your friend is. Just because you don't have something you want right now, it doesn't mean that you won't get it in the future. Do your best to be happy for your friend

12 Becoming Overwhelmed

Going to movies, bowling, picnics, and school events can be fun. But these can also be loud and overwhelming events. If you tend to feel overwhelmed in situations like these, it is best to have a plan. The plan can be a secret signal or a secret word that you can use with your parents or another adult who is with you to say that you need a break. Another plan might be to bring things with that give you a break without having to leave, such as noise-canceling headphones, earplugs, a good book, an iPod with music … No matter what works for you, it is always best to have a plan.

13 Solving Problems

Every problem has an answer. Sometimes you might not know the answer, and that is okay. The two most important things that you should keep in mind are knowing who to ask when there is a problem and then not to be afraid to ask. Most of the time your parents, teachers, or some other adult can help you find the answer.

Here's a quick chart that helps you solve a problem. Your parents or teacher can help you learn how to do this.

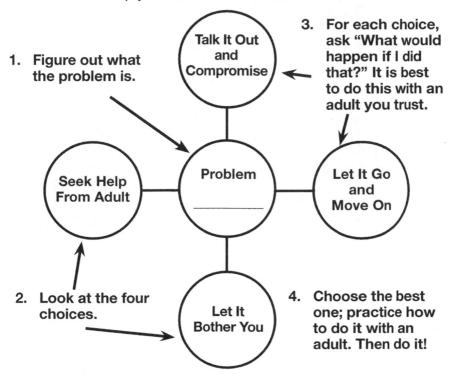

1. **Figure out what the problem is.**

3. **For each choice, ask "What would happen if I did that?" It is best to do this with an adult you trust.**

2. **Look at the four choices.**

4. **Choose the best one; practice how to do it with an adult. Then do it!**

Chart circles: Talk It Out and Compromise — Problem — Seek Help From Adult — Let It Go and Move On — Let It Bother You

14 GETTING A HANDLE ON HOW YOU ARE FEELING

Sometimes we get upset over things that might not really be a big deal. But it can be hard to tell the "big" things from the "small" things. Here is something to help people get a handle on how they are feeling. It is called the Incredible 5-Point Scale. The Incredible 5-Point Scale is really easy to use. You can make a scale with your parents or teacher for the kind of situations that you find hard.

1. **Make a table.**
2. **Label the top columns.**
3. **Write numbers down the side.**
4. **Write in your feelings for each number.**
5. **Write down what each feeling looks like for you.**
6. **Write what you should do for each number.**

Rating	Feeling	What It Looks Like	What You Should Do
5	I have to leave; it is time to be alone.	Fast rocking; loud voice	Use the secret signal with the adult you trust and leave the room when the adult acknowledges you.
4	I need to move to a different place in the room.	Rocking back and forth; picking on my fingernails	Say, "Excuse me," if you can. If you can't, just walk to a quiet part of the room and put on your headphones. Think about using your secret signal with an adult.
3	I need to stop talking with this person or I might need help telling someone to be quiet.	Feeling like I want to flap my hands and cover my ears	Think about saying one of these things, "I'll talk with you later," "I'm going to get a drink," "I need to get some work done." If that is not going to work, say "Gotta go!" and go stand by an adult you like and know. Ask the adult for help.
2	I can do this by myself.	Starting to tap my foot	Take a deep breath and count to 10. Think about saying one of these things, "I'll talk with you later," "I'm going to get a drink," "I need to get some work done."
1	I am good. Nothing is really bothering me.	Smiling, talking	Keep doing what I am doing.

First Aid

See also CALLING "911"

1 IF YOU GET A CUT

If you get a regular, everyday cut or scrape, rinse it with warm water and put a Band-Aid on it. If it is a bad and deep cut, tell your mom, dad, or other adult. If necessary, they will take you to the emergency room or call "911" for an ambulance.

2 SICK PET

If you think your pet is sick, tell your parents or another adult. Let your pet rest and put his food and water bowls by his bed. Call the veterinarian and ask for tips or medicines to cure your pet. Follow your veterinarian's advice and check your pet every 30 minutes or so to see how he is doing.

3 SPLINTER

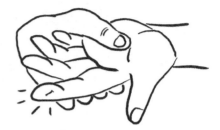

If you get a splinter, tell an adult. The adult will probably numb it with ice and try to pull it out with a pair of tweezers. If it hurts too much when you put the tweezers on it, you and your parents might decide to let it fall out by itself. Watch to make sure that the area does not get infected by cleaning it carefully and maybe putting some medication on it. An adult can help you do this.

4 BITES

If chiggers bite you, don't panic. Ask an adult for some medication to stop the itch, and don't make it worse by scratching, even if that is very tempting. If you have no medication available, clear fingernail polish usually works. Sometimes soaking in an oatmeal bath can also stop the itching. But regardless of what you try, be sure to ask an adult for help.

If a dog or some other animal bites you and breaks the skin, tell your parents or another adult immediately. Ask the person who owns the animal if it has had a rabies shot. If not, or if there is no owner around, you need to see your doctor as soon as possible to get checked out and possibly get a tetanus shot. If the animal bite does not break through the skin, there is usually nothing to worry about. Anyway, always tell your parents and wash the area carefully.

5 BROKEN BONES

If you ever see someone and you think he has broken a bone, tell an adult as the person will need to go to the doctor or the emergency room. If there is no adult around, call "911." If you get hurt yourself and think you have a broken bone, stay where you are and call out for an adult to find you. Be prepared to go to a hospital for x-rays and other treatment.

6 CHOKING

If you are ever choking, make the universal sign for choking, or if you are able to talk, tell others around you that you are choking. If someone else is choking, yell out and get an adult as quickly as possible to do the Heimlich maneuver. This is a special way to help people who are choking; to do the Heimlich maneuver a person has to be specially trained.

7 IF YOU LOSE A TOOTH

If your tooth falls out, wash your mouth out with water, if possible. If you want to save your tooth, clean it and get a small plastic bag, if available, to put it in. Let your parents know that you lost a tooth.

If one of your teeth is knocked out, immediately tell an adult as you will probably have to go to the dentist. If possible, save the tooth and take it with you to the dentist.

8 INFECTION

If you think you have an infection, tell your mom or dad, so they can arrange a doctor's appointment, if necessary. An infection can be a rash or red bumps that irritate your skin, a sore with a red circle around it, or a sore with pus coming out.

9 NOSE BLEED

If you ever have a nosebleed, don't panic. It happens to most people at one time or another. To help stop the bleeding, hold your head high in the air and pinch the very top part of your nose. Wash the blood away. Make sure you find your parents, teacher or other adult and tell them your nose is bleeding.

10 IF YOUR FEET HURT

If your feet hurt, tell your parents to take a look. Your shoes may be too small, your shoes might not be built right for your feet, or maybe you have a bruise. Keep your toenails cut square because if you don't, you might get an ingrown toenail, and that can make your feet hurt too.

11 INJURED ANIMAL

If you come across an injured animal, don't push or touch it. Stay away, because injured animals will run or fight if someone gets too close. If an adult is with you, one of you should call the owner or Animal Control.

12 STINGS

If a wasp stings you, tell an adult. The adult will usually find some kind of medicine, spray or cream that can make it feel better. If you are allergic to bees or wasps, find an adult immediately. You may have to go to the doctor and get a special prescription.

13 WHAT TO DO IF YOU FIND SOMEONE WHO IS HURT

If you find someone who is hurt, ask if she is all right. If the person has a skinned knee or elbow, help her get up and take her somewhere to get the area washed and get a Band-Aid. If you don't know what to do, comfort the person until help arrives. If it looks like a serious injury, never try to move the person as it could make the injury even worse.

Miscellaneous

GETTING LOST IN A STORE

If you get separated from your family in a store, go to the checkout register and ask for help. Tell the cashier your family member's or other adult's name, and describe what he or she looks like. Some families have a certain spot they go to when they are lost. My friend Ivy and her family always go to the back right-hand corner of the store and wait for each other if one of them gets lost. It is important not to panic and not to go with anyone who is not your family member. The only exception would be to ask a person who works in the store for help.

2 SHARING THINGS WITH YOUR BROTHER OR SISTER

Try not to fight or argue about toys, games, or other things. If you have something that is very important to you, ask your mom and dad if it is necessary to share it with others. If they tell you to share, tell your brother or sister that you want to play with your toy first for at least 10 minutes, and then they can use it for 10 minutes after that. You might want to set a timer to keep track of the time to make sure it's fair.

3 WANTING TO STAY UP LATE

If you want to stay up late, it is best to do it on Fridays and Saturdays so you won't get too tired on school days. If you want to stay up late on school days, ask your parents for permission. If it's okay, set your alarm clock so you can wake up on time in the morning.

4 IF YOU ARE LOCKED OUT OF YOUR HOUSE

If you have an automatic garage door opener, make sure you know the code. The code is usually something that is easy to remember by everybody in your family, such as a holiday or somebody's birthday. Keep a piece of paper with the code on it in your backpack to help you remember but make sure the note doesn't say "garage door code." You might also want to talk to your parents about giving a key to your neighbor so you can go to the neighbor's house and borrow it if you are locked out. Remember to return the key for future use.

5 IF YOU CAN'T FIND SOMETHING YOU ARE LOOKING FOR

If you cannot find something you are looking for, remain calm. Try to think of the last place you had the item. If you start to get upset, think about something else or do something else for about 10 minutes. Then try to look for it again. You may also want to ask an adult, brother, sister, or friend to help you look. Also, if you put things in their correct place when you are done with them, you probably will not have this problem very often.

6 IF YOU GET HUNGRY

If you get hungry, fix yourself something simple. Follow the rules your family has for what appliances you can use if an adult isn't home and what foods you can eat. Eating cereal is almost always a good idea, especially when you can't think of anything else.

7 HOME ALONE

If you are home alone, make sure you have all of the necessary phone numbers (business, cell phone, etc.) so you can get ahold of your parents or other adult in case you need them. Try not to think about your parents too often because that might make you feel sad. Play games, be safe, and have fun! You might also want to call a friend on the telephone, if it is okay with your parents. Don't invite anyone over unless you have permission to do so. Keep your doors locked.

8 IF YOU ARE LONESOME

If you are lonesome, ask your parents if you can call one of your friends. If you are still lonely after hanging up the phone, ask your parents if one of your friends can come over and play. If they say no, ask if your parents or other family members want to play a board game with you, swing, read a book, etc., etc. Have fun!

9 HOW TO KEEP YOURSELF BUSY IN A CAR OR ON AN AIRPLANE

Plan ahead for your trip. Choose small things like a coloring book and crayons, an MP3 player with head-phones, books, travel-size games, crossword puzzles, and magazines to pack in a backpack or small suitcase that you can take with you. If your parent brings a lap-top computer, you can ask if you may use it. You can use the laptop with music CDs, DVDs, and computer games. My mom usually buys me one or two small things that I have not played with before so I can have something to do on the trip.

10 IF YOUR PET GETS LOST

If your pet is lost, tell your mom or dad as soon as possible. Also call the animal pound to let them know. Tell them where you live, your phone number, and your pet's name. You might also want to make a poster about your pet and put it up in your neighborhood. If possible, the poster should have a picture of your pet, a description of your pet, your pet's name, directions for what to do if someone finds your pet, and your phone number. In most cases, pets are soon found.

11 PICKING UP YOUR TOYS

If you don't pick your toys off the floor, the "toy fairy" may come and take them away in the middle of the night. You, or somebody else, also might trip over the toys and get hurt, or you may forget where your toys are the next time you want to play with them. If you don't always want to pick up your toys immediately after you have played with them, ask your parents if there is a place where you can leave them out for a while. I have a little playroom where I can leave things out for a while. No matter what, it is best to clean up your toys every day because if you don't, it becomes a big mess and then it takes even longer to clean up.

12 IF YOU FIND SOMETHING THAT DOES NOT BELONG TO YOU

If you find something that doesn't belong to you in a store, restaurant, movie theater or some other place, take it to the nearest Lost and Found. If you find something on the street, ask the person closest to you if he or she lost something. All you need to say is, "Did you lose anything?" You don't want to give all of the details about the item. If the person answers yes, ask him or her to describe what the lost item is to be sure this is the rightful owner.

13 BEDWETTING

If you happen to wet your bed, don't worry. Many kids have this problem. Avoid drinking liquids late in the day and go to the bathroom right before you go to bed. If you do wet the bed, tell your mom or dad immediately so they can help you put on clean sheets and covers.

14 TROUBLE FINDING THINGS OR BEING ORGANIZED

If you lose a worksheet, ask the teacher for another one. Don't get upset. Try to put things away in the same place each time after you use them. Sometimes a special notebook, like Intelligear, can help you organize your schoolwork. I have baskets in my bedroom. Each one is for a certain type of toy or book. I put my hair things in one basket and my Password Journal in another. I keep most of my Egyptian stuff on one shelf so I know where it is.

15 SOMETHING BOTHERS YOUR SENSES

If you are outside and the sun is too bright, go inside or wear sunglasses. If you are inside and the light is too bright, ask your teacher or parents if you can turn out the lights and open the shades.

If it is too warm and you are wearing a sweater, take off the sweater. If you are still too warm, ask your teacher or parents to lower the temperature.

If a sound is hurting your ears, you might want to wear earplugs. Ask your parents if you can carry earplugs with you wherever you go if a lot of sounds bother you.

If you are a picky eater, make sure that you have something you like to eat. I am a picky eater and I always have a snack with me just in case I get hungry.

16 SOMEONE ASKS YOU TO DO SOMETHING MEAN OR BAD

If someone asks you to do something mean or bad to someone else, say "No, it is wrong to hurt kids or hurt their feelings." Someone who asks you to do something wrong is not a friend because friends would not do that to each other.

17 BATHROOM PROTOCOL

Using public restrooms can pose problems.

- When trying to find an empty stall in a crowded restroom, don't look between the cracks separating the stalls. Instead, look slightly underneath the stall door just so you can see a person's feet. If you find an empty stall, you can use it.

- Before using the toilet, always make sure that the stall door is closed and locked and that there is toilet paper.

- If you accidentally spill on the toilet seat, just take some clean toilet paper and clean it up. When finished, flush the toilet, pull up your pants, and wash your hands with soap and water.

- When in a public restroom, it is not a good idea to talk to others unless you know them. Girls may talk to the person in the next stall over if she is a good friend. Also, if you have no toilet paper, it is okay to put your hand under the stall next to yours and ask if the person has any extra toilet paper, even if you are in a restroom with strangers.

- Boys don't normally talk to each other in a restroom. If you are a boy, always check the stall for toilent paper before you go to the bathroom.

18 AT THE DOCTOR'S OFFICE

When you are at the doctor's office, people get upset if you ask them why they are there, and they might be grossed out if you tell them why you are there. It is best to leave other people alone in the waiting room and just tell the doctor why you are there.

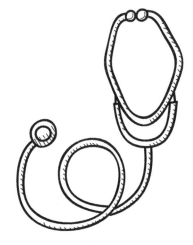

19 WAITING IN LINE

If you are waiting in line for something, you are not allowed to cut in, no matter how long you have been waiting. The people in front of you have been waiting longer than you. Instead, try to pass the time by playing little games, like counting the ceiling tiles or the people in blue shirts; you could also "write" a story in your head. You will find that the time will seem to pass much faster that way.

Your Own Ideas

Use the following pages to add your own ideas for hidden curriculum items.

School-Related

Getting Along

_____

_____

_____

_____

_____

_____

_____

_____

_____

_____

_____

Emotions and Concerns

First Aid

Miscellaneous

Other Books From AAPC for Elementary-Age Children

Totally Chill: My Complete Guide to Staying Cool

A Stress Management Workbook for Kids With Social, Emotional, or Sensory Sensitivities

by Christopher Lynch, PhD

Code 9079 | Price: $22.00

My Sensory Book:

Working Together to Explore Sensory Issues and the Big Feelings They Can Cause: A Workbook for Parents, Professionals, and Children

by Lauren H. Kerstein, LCSW

Code 9006 | Price: $22.00

Why Does Izzy Cover Her Ears?

Dealing With Sensory Overload

written and illustrated by Jennifer Veenendall

Code 9037 | Price: $19.00

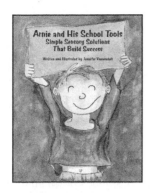

Arnie and His School Tools:

Simple Sensory Solutions That Build Success

written and illustrated by Jennifer Veenendall

Code 9002 | Price: $19.00

Out and About

Preparing Children With Autism Spectrum Disorders to Participate in Their Communities

by Jill Hudson and Amy Bixler Coffin

Code 9991 | Price: $20.00

My New School:

A Workbook to Help Students Transition to a New School

by Melissa L. Trautman, MsEd; foreword by Brenda Smith Myles, PhD

Code 9054 | Price: $20.00

Diary of a Social Detective –

Real-Life Tales of Mystery, Intrigue and Interpersonal Adventure

by Jeffrey E. Jessum, PhD

Code 9063 | Price: $20.00

More Advance Praise....

"This truly is the 'Mother's Little Helper' of the autism community! No more struggling to think of spontaneous explanations or reminders. Put one copy of the book in your child's backpack and another under his pillow! Few things I've seen will foster more independence in children with high-functioning autism than *The Hidden Curriculum and Other Everyday Challenges for Children with High-Functioning Autism*."
  – Sherry Moyer, executive/research director, the University of Toledo Center for Excellence in Autism

"This book is a good match for me! It's organized by topic, easy to understand, and full of useful information. I keep it on my bookshelf and look things up when I don't know how to act or what to do in different situations."
  – Kaede Sakai, 13 years old and in 7th grade at Cal Young Middle School; she has a chihuahua named Lulu

"As the father of a teenage daughter with Asperger Syndrome, I highly recommend this book. Since she began studying the hidden curriculum, I have seen her effectively manage meeting new people, respond to compliments, display good manners, and appropriately express anxiety. The teachings have given her tools to help her get past the first awkward moments of an encounter and a chance to engage others."
  – Charles Evans, father of teenager with high-functioning autism

"We have been using books on the hidden curriculum during individual and group services for years, with many students reading the books and calendars cover to cover. We are very excited about the new and expanded edition, *The Hidden Curriculum and Other Everyday Challenges for Elementary-Age Children With High-Functioning Autism*. This easy-to-read book provides examples from a child's perspective on a variety of topics we often forget to teach. What I especially like about it is its ability to encourage students to think of options of what to do in a given situation, which is not an easy skill for most students with ASD. Great resource for any classroom or home."
  – Kerry Mataya, MSEd, author of *Successful Problem-Solving for High-Functioning Students With Autism Spectrum Disorders* and director and consultant for the Autism Asperger Syndrome Consulting Group, LLC, in the Birmingham, Alabama area, providing educational consultation to local school systems, behavior programming, after-school social groups, and summer camps

AAPC
PUBLISHING

P.O. Box 23173
Shawnee Mission, Kansas 66283-0173
www.aapcpublishing.net

CPSIA information can be obtained at www.ICGtesting.com
Printed in the USA
LVOW04s1948190415

435236LV00002B/3/P